Learning From God's Birds

By Ruth Johnson Jay

Illustrated by Lynette Ratzlaff

Copyright © 1981
by Bethel Publishing, Elkhart, IN 46516
All Rights Reserved.
ISBN 0-934998-05-1
Litho in U.S.A.

Scripture quotations are from
the New International Version, © 1978
by N.Y. International Bible Society.
Used by Permission.

This book, **Learning from God's Birds,** is designed to help **preschool** age children gain more knowledge about God's creations. Through this information, the child's mind is then directed to see the God of these creations.

This material can be used at bedtime, during morning devotionals, or as a supplement to Sunday School, Vacation Bible School, or Good News Club lessons.

Scriptures are taken from the New International Version of the Bible. They are purposely made to be very short, to encourage the young child to memorize them.

It is the hope and prayer of this author that God will use this book to open up new and wonderful spiritual truths to the **preschool** age child.

Ruth Johnson Jay, author

Bee Eaters and Growing Up

How would you like the job of having to run down the road trying to catch a chicken or something else before you could have something to eat? That would be hard work, wouldn't it? You would get awfully hungry before you caught it and had it fixed for dinner. It is much better to have Mother go to the supermarket and buy the food, isn't it?

There is a bird who must chase after his dinner. When he sees something special flying around in the air, he knows he will soon be eating. Even the young bird must do this. It is the bee eater.

This bird has a long, pointed beak. This is what he uses to get his food. And what is his favorite dinner? Bees! That is why he is called the bee eater.

Before the bee eater actually gets his dinner, he sits quietly on a bush, a post, or a telephone wire. He keeps his eye on everything that is going on. When he sees a swarm of bees begin to fly, he goes into action. Bravely he attacks the bees and gets one into his bill. Then he takes his catch back to his perch. There he slams it against a limb, beating it until it no longer moves. Now he can finally gulp down his dinner.

The young bee eater learns quickly how to make his catch without allowing one of the bees to sting him. The older he gets, the better he becomes at his job.

The older you get, the better you will become at living like Jesus wants you to live. And how does He want you to live? The Bible says you are to be kind, loving, truthful, and good.

Are you?

"Live at peace with everyone"
(Romans 12:18).

WHITE-THROATED BEE EATER

Birds and God's House

Everyone has a certain place to live. We call it a house or a home. Birds have certain homes too. Some birds stay in the same area all year-round. When they do, they keep the same house all of their lives. Other birds migrate to warmer climates. Those birds have one house for the summer and another one for the winter.

When birds fly to their new homes, they always have a leader. He is like a boss. When they finally arrive at their homes, they set up property lines just like people do. The male bird calls for the female bird to come and join him in his house. If she comes, this place then becomes their property forever. Sometimes a younger bird takes what another bird has had first. When this happens, the older bird pushes him out until he leaves and gives the property back to the original owner.

The female bird is attracted to her mate through voice and food. First she listens as the male bird calls to her. But before she joins him, she checks to see that there will be food. If everything looks all right, she stays.

The female bird builds the nests. If she happens to get into a tree that belongs to a bird other than her mate, he will never come to that nest. Instead, he will keep calling until she leaves and brings her young to the place that belongs to her mate.

So birds have their own territories. They know exactly where to go when they arrive. Christians should know where to go too. One thing the Bible tells us is that we should go to the house of the Lord. That is the church. Do you go to church and Sunday school every week? If not, be sure to start this week. It is very good to make God's house part of your territory.

"Let us go to the house of the Lord" (Psalm 122:1).

CAROLINA WREN

AMERICAN GOLDEN PLOVER

Birds and Miracles

Those who have studied the life and habits of birds say that these little creatures are "great miracles."

Just before a bird begins his Fall migration (that is the time when he travels to other climates), the old worn out feathers drop off. New feathers grow in and take their place. This way, the bird will be able to fly long distances without any feather problems.

Some birds can fly 5000 feet in the air. This is one of the reasons bird watchers call them "great miracles." For instance, a tiny black pole warbler who may have his summer nest in Canada, suddenly leaves and goes to Brazil, four thousand miles away. He knows exactly where to go and how to get there. That is a miracle. The golden plover travels 8000 miles on his trip to Argentina. He too knows where he is going.

Yes, it is a great miracle the way these and other birds know when to leave, where to go, and how to get there. But there are some miracles that are even bigger than these. They are the miracles of God.

When God created the world, He made it out of nothing. That was a great miracle. When Jesus attended a wedding one day, He made water become wine. Another time when Jesus talked to Nicodemus, He told the man that he needed to be born again. And to be born again is a great miracle.

But the greatest miracle of all was when Jesus left heaven and came to die for the sins of the whole world. By doing that, He brought salvation for everyone who will ever believe. Have you believed? Are you a part of this miracle?

"God so loved the world" (John 3:16).

Cranes and Quarrels

The crane is a large, long-legged bird. It is the tallest of all the wading birds. It stands about four or five feet high and looks like a stork. The crane has a long neck. When it flies, it holds both its neck and head straight forward. Legs and feet are held straight behind. With wings stretched out, the crane almost looks like an airplane.

Cranes eat both animals and vegetables. They especially like grasshoppers and crickets. (How would you like a grasshopper or cricket dinner?) Cranes can eat four or five hundred of them at one time.

In some parts of the world cranes have been known to damage the wheat crops. So farmers do not like to see them on their farms.

Baby cranes can stand and walk when they are just a few hours old. As brother and sister cranes start growing up, they do what children sometimes do. They quarrel. First one of the little cranes starts to peck at the other one, and soon they are both pecking at each other. They do this as long as one or the other can take it. Finally one gets tired of putting up with that kind of treatment and leaves home. When this happens, that little crane is usually lost forever.

In the Old Testament we read about Joseph and his brothers. The older brothers did not treat Joseph very well. One day they sold him as a slave. Then they went home and told their father that Joseph was lost, that he had probably been killed by a wild animal. But God was with Joseph. He took care of him, and made him a great ruler.

Are there brothers or sisters in your family? God wants you to love them, to be kind to them, and to treat them well.

"Keep on loving each other" (Hebrews 13:1).

WHOOPING CRANE

SCREECH OWL

Birds and God's Creation

Did you know that God made His very special kind of airplane? He did this long before any man thought to make our kind of airplane. He called it a bird.

When God made birds, He gave them something He did not even give to people. He gave them wings. God knew that birds would fly in the sky, so for that very reason He gave them wings. Because birds must fly, they cannot be heavy. So God made them light, but with strong and powerful wings.

God also knew that if a bird were going to fly around in the sky and still get his food from down on the ground, he would have to have good eyesight. So God gave him large eyeballs. Birds, like hawks or owls, have outstanding eyesight. A hawk can see more than a mile away.

Some birds can fly up to a hundred miles an hour, and then suddenly swoop down to a complete stop on the ground. They do this especially if they spot some food in the distance.

Birds do not have teeth. They don't need them. If birds had teeth, they would also need jaws and muscles to take care of the teeth. But all this would make birds too heavy to be good fliers. So God did not give them teeth.

Birds are made in a wonderful way. And they are made by a wonderful God. The same God who made birds, made us. And when He did, He gave us something He did not give to a bird. He gave us a heart and a mind so that we can love Him.

God is so good.

"God saw that it was good" (Genesis 1:10).

Cormorants and Fishing

A cormorant is a long necked, long billed, diving bird. He is usually black in color or sometimes black mixed with some blue and green. His feet are large and webbed. Webbed means that there is no separation between the toes. It is this webbing that helps him to be such a good swimmer.

The cormorant's main food is fish. He dives into the water to find his food. His wings are used for steering and braking. When the cormorant finds his fish, he gets it into his mouth but does not eat it immediately. Instead, he brings it to the surface and there he swallows it.

Cormorants sometimes make it very hard for people who fish for a living. If the cormorant sees the fish before a fisherman gets to it, it is impossible for the man to make his catch.

On the other hand, the cormorant is sometimes very useful to the fisherman. In China and Japan, fishermen fit a ring around the cormorant's neck so that when he gets the fish in his mouth and begins to surface, that is all he can do. Because of the ring he cannot swallow his catch. The fisherman then takes the fish and sends the bird down again to bring up even more fish.

Jesus' disciples were fishermen. Sometimes they caught lots of fish and sometimes they caught nothing. One time when their boat was sitting on the shore, Jesus sat in it and taught the people who had come to hear Him. After that, He told the disciples to put down their nets and when they did, they had a whole net full of fish.

When Jesus is near, everything goes well. The disciples learned this and we should too.

"Let down the nets for a catch" (Luke 5:4).

GREAT CORMORANT

10

CRAB-PLOVER

Crab-Plovers and a Name

The crab-plover is a white bird with a black beak and feathers. His bill is almost like a dagger. The crab-plover got his name from the fact that crabs are his main food. Because he has such a dagger-like bill, he can crack the tough shells of the crabs with almost no effort at all.

The crab-plover is a very restless bird. Sometimes as he is eating his meal, he suddenly stops, flies out over the water and then comes back to finish eating.

Crab-plovers nest in colonies. Often hundreds of pairs are seen together near the sea. If a hunter happens to shoot a crab-plover, all the other members of the flock will gather around, make loud noises and follow the hunter wherever he goes.

Just as the crab-plover has a name that shows he eats crabs, so Christians have a name to show that they are followers of Christ.

When Jesus began His ministry on earth, He called certain people to become His followers. He saw James and John out in a boat. They were fishing. He called to them and asked them to follow Him. James and John obeyed Jesus. They left their fishing gear and became two of Jesus' disciples.

Matthew was a tax collector. Jesus asked him to be a follower too. Matthew left his work and he too became a disciple of Jesus.

We should follow Him too.

"I will follow you" (Luke 9:57).

Babblers and Singing

GRAY-CROWNED SCIMITAR BABBLER

Have you ever been called a babbler? If so, it was probably because you were being noisy or talking too much.

A babbler is the name of a bird. It is a very pretty bird, but a noisy one. There are many different kinds of babblers. One of them is called the song babbler. Most babblers eat insects. But the song babbler is different; he looks for fruit.

The song babbler has become a favorite as a "cage" bird. That means that people like to have one in their home. But they cannot let this bird fly all over the house, so they keep him in a cage.

Say, what kind of babbler are you? Are you the noisy kind who goes around making lots of loud sounds? Or are you like the song babbler, one who brings happiness because you sing with real joy?

Lots of people make noise; only a few make music. But Jesus wants all of us to be like the song babbler, singing songs about Him.

In the book of Psalms there are many verses that tell us to sing. Here are some of those reminders.

"Sing praises to the Lord" (Ps. 9:11).
"Sing joyfully to the Lord" (Ps. 33:1).
"Sing to Him a new song" (Ps. 33:3).
"Sing praises to our king" (Ps. 47:6).
"Sing for joy to God" (Ps. 81:1).

So if you must be a babbler, be sure you are not a noisy one, but instead a happy song babbler.

Choose any of these verses to memorize.

Emus and No Mistakes

If you lived in Australia, you would no doubt see a very large bird that looks something like an ostrich. This bird is the Emu. He weighs about eighty or ninety pounds and is just about as tall as an adult person.

The Emu is brown. His feathers form a loose hair-like covering on his body. His legs do not have any feathers on them. The Emu's legs are so long that he can easily take a step that is nine feet long. (Why don't you take a big step and see how long it is. It won't be as long as the Emu's.)

The Emu has three toes on each foot. He has a broad, soft bill so he can graze and find food. The adult Emu feeds mainly on fruit, flowers, insects, and seeds. When he can find caterpillars and grasshoppers, he will eat great numbers of those too.

The Emu has wings, but he does not fly. Now, why would God put wings on this bird when he was not going to be able to fly? Remember, God never makes any mistakes, so there has to be a reason for the wings. And there is.

The Emu's wings are very important to him, especially in the hot weather. When he needs to cool off, he simply holds his wings out so that the air can refresh his body and make him feel good. Yes, God gave the Emu wings so they could be used like a fan.

Isn't God wonderful? He even thought about keeping the Emu comfortable. But then this should not surprise us, because God does everything right. He is perfect. When He created the world, He did not make birds until He had first made trees, so they would have a place to build nests for their young. God does everything just right.

"As for God, his way is perfect" (Psalm 18:30).

EMU

PEREGRINE FALCON

Falcons and Food

The falcon looks like certain other birds. It has a hooked beak just like the eagle or hawk. This bird has short wings and a long tail. It also has very good eyes.

Falcons are found in many parts of the world. They attack smaller animals and other birds and also eat snakes and bugs. Sometimes they make their catch while they are flying in the air.

Falcons can kill other animals with their feet or bills. When they eat, they often stuff themselves with lots of food. Then they may not eat again for a long time.

People cannot do that. God made our bodies so that we need to eat often and digest our food slowly. And even when we eat a lot of food, we still get hungry again.

Even Jesus became hungry. He had to have food just like we do. One day while He was leaving the city of Bethany, He became hungry. There was a fig tree not too far away. Jesus went over to the tree so He could pick some figs. But when He got there, the tree was empty. There were no figs on it. He did not get the food He was looking for and needed.

The Bible is sometimes called "food." Bible-food makes us strong and healthy as children of the Lord. Maybe you are not old enough to read the Bible for yourself. But you are old enough to listen when it is being read. And you are old enough to learn some of the verses from the Bible too. Are you doing it?

"All your words are true" (Psalm 119:160).

Flamingos and Beauty

The flamingo is one of the most beautiful birds you will ever see. Most of them live in the tropical countries. (That is where it is very warm.) Maybe you have seen one in the zoo. This bird is colored with a mixture of pink, red, and black. The colors are bright and beautiful.

Flamingos are usually seen on the shoreline or riverbanks. The reason they are there is because this is where they can find their food. They wade into the shallow water and find food there too.

AMERICAN FLAMINGO

Even though flamingos are such beautiful birds, there is one thing about them that is not so beautiful—their voices. They are loud-sounding and not musical at all. But this not-so-pretty voice is very useful. It is used to keep the group together.

In some ways flamingos are "show-off" birds. When large groups gather together, they go through a parade-like exercise. First they stand up very straight. Then together they all proudly stretch themselves before they stand straight again. After this they wag their heads in all directions. Now comes a beautiful sight. Together they spread their wings and then fold them back once again.

Flamingos also march together in a large group. They can march forward or backward. But they also always do it together. This is usually done to attract the attention of other birds.

And who made this beautiful flamingo? God did. But God did not only make this beautiful bird, He made people too. He made you. Yes, you are one of God's beautiful creations.

"He has made everything beautiful" (Ecclesiastes 3:11).

LAUGHING GULL

Gulls and Groups

If you have been around a lakeshore or seaside, you may have seen the sea gulls walking or flying around. These birds are gray and white and have long wings. These wings are helpful as they fly around or as they soar high into the air.

Gulls do not dive deep into the water to find food like some birds do. Instead they dip into the shallow parts. They feed mostly on fish or smaller birds and eggs and will stay around in one place as long as food or garbage can be found. Sometimes when they are no longer hungry, they will pick up the garbage and take it back to their nests. Because the gulls pick up garbage and bad food and carry it around, they are responsible for carrying around lots of diseases too. This is not good.

Gulls build their nests wherever there is food. So if food is scarce, you will only find one or two nests in a group. Other times when there is much food, there will be as many as several thousand nests together.

When Jesus taught the people, sometimes He would talk to hundreds of them. Other times, He would just talk to one or two people at a time. One time when He was walking down a busy road, crowds of people followed Him. They wanted to see Him. But there was one man who was not able to see Jesus. He was too short. And there were too many people in the way. So this man, Zacchaeus, decided to climb a tree and wait for Jesus to come by. Jesus looked up and saw Zacchaeus and then invited Himself to the man's house. Jesus had seen the crowd, but He had seen Zacchaeus too.

Jesus sees everything and everyone. He sees the thousands of nests that the sea gulls make and He sees all people wherever they are. He sees you too. God is so great.

"The Son of Man came to seek and to save" (Luke 19:10).

Hammerheads and Homes

Unless you live in Africa you have probably never seen the bird that is called a hammerhead. It is a very unusual looking bird. It has a large, long bill with a small hook on the end. The hammerhead's long legs have four toes. Three of them point forward and one points to the back.

Some of the people in Africa are afraid of this little bird. They say they will have bad luck if they do anything to harm the hammerhead. So they are very careful to treat it well.

Hammerheads are often seen wading around in the shallow water. They shuffle their feet as they walk. This is the way they search for hidden food. Their diet is usually fish, though the young hammerheads will eat tadpoles.

Sometimes these birds can be seen jumping on the back of a big hippopotamus. It does this so it can use the animal's back as a platform. Then it tries to spot more food.

It takes the hammerhead a long time to build a nest. First the bird looks for a fork in the tree. Then it gets sticks. With dry mud, the hammerhead puts things together and makes the nest. This takes about six months.

God is building a mansion in heaven for believers. Did you know that? When life is all over, Christians will go to heaven to be with Jesus. Then we will see the mansion that Jesus has built for us.

But only those who have come to Jesus to be forgiven of sin will have that mansion. If you have believed on Jesus and asked Him to make you His child, then you too will have a mansion in heaven and live forever and ever with God.

"I go and prepare a place for you" (John 14:3).

HAMMERHEAD

GREATER HONEYGUIDE

Honey Guides and Honey People

Have you ever heard of a bird that is called the honey guide? It is a small, dull brown bird. It looks something like a woodpecker. Most honey guides are found in Africa, so you may never have seen one.

When the female honey guide lays her eggs, she goes to a nest that has been built by a woodpecker, a starling, or some other bird. If there are already some eggs in that nest, the honey guide destroys those eggs, and then lays her own eggs in that same nest. In this action the honey guide is not a very nice bird.

But the honey guide does some good things too. As the name shows, honey guides will guide people or other animals to the place where honey can be found. Because these birds have such thick skin, they can go into the bees' nests and not get hurt even if they get stung. When they find a nest, they call out loudly until they get the attention of the person or animal looking for the honey. If the people or animals are slow in arriving, the honey guide flies back, still calling and then again leads the way to the honey.

After the honeycombs have been opened and the honey taken out, the bird then eats the wax. This is a most unusual thing for a bird to do. The honey guide seems to be able to digest it.

Children can act like the honey guide. Sometimes they are very kind and helpful, other times unkind and pouty. Jesus wants you to show kindness to your mother and father, to those you play with, and even to those who are not kind to you.

Don't be a honey guide person; be kind always. Be like Jesus who loves everyone at all times.

"Love does not delight in evil" (I Corinthians 13:6).

Loons and Crying

The loon is sometimes called a diver. It has no tail, but it does have a long neck and a pointed beak. The legs of the loon are so far back on the body that it is almost impossible for him to walk around. But walking is not as important to the loon as swimming. He is an excellent swimmer, probably the best in the whole bird kingdom.

There are many different kinds of loons: the black throated loon, the red throated loon, the white billed loon and one called the common loon. He has this name because he is so common around the country. But no matter what their names or where they live, all loons eat fish. Because of this, they have to be very good at diving. (Do you see why he is called a diver?) Sometimes a loon dives thirty feet into the water. He may stay down as long as two minutes at a time. Finally he comes up with his prized fish. He can swim so fast under water that he catches his fish while he is swimming. Loons eat frogs, worms, and water insects too.

The baby loon leaves the nest after about one or two days. He can swim right away. He goes out into the water and meets his mother and father. He knows they will have some food for him. Even though the baby loon can swim right after he is born, it takes about sixty days before he can fly.

The loon has a cry that is different from almost any other bird. It sounds like a little child screaming when he has been hurt. Some people have been fooled when they hear the loon cry. They think there is a little baby somewhere.

In the Bible the word "crying" sometimes means praying or talking to God. God hears when you "cry" to Him. He knows when you are calling on Him to help you. So when He hears your "cry" (that is, your prayers) He always answers. Isn't God wonderful?

"I cry out to God" (Psalm 57:2).

ARCTIC LOON

MASKED LOVEBIRD

Lovebirds and Actions

The lovebird is actually an African parrot, but this name is sometimes given to other birds as well. The true lovebird is only about four inches long, has a short tail, and is found in Ethiopia and other African countries. These birds are mainly green in color, but the female's head is also a yellow-green.

Lovebirds were given this name because they show so much love and attention to their mates. Sometimes it is only the male who shows special attention to his female. She does not return his care and attention. But other birds are different. Attention and love are shown by both the male and the female.

The lovebird can also be a good fighter. Sometimes these fights turn into games to see which bird can bite the other bird's foot first.

The word lovebird is also given to people who show love, care, and concern for each other. Wouldn't it be nice if all Christians would be called lovebirds because they care about others?

Christians should show love, because love is the main theme of the Bible. God loved us so much that He gave Jesus to be our Saviour. He loves us and we should love Him.

The Bible also tells us that we should love one another; that means we should love people we know, like our parents, sisters, brothers, and friends. The Bible even tells us that we should love our enemies.

Are you the kind of person that God sees as one of His lovebirds? You should be. He loved, and He wants you to love too.

"Faith, hope and love. The greatest . . . is love" (I Corinthians 13:13).

Mockingbirds and Family

Can you think of a bird that lives in the southern part of the United States that is known for imitating other birds? He can change his song not only to sound like other birds, but like a hen or even a frog.

Most other birds do their singing during the daytime; this bird sings during the day and also at night. This is especially true during the breeding season. Do you know the name of this bird?

Yes, it is the mockingbird. He was given his name because he was able to imitate other sounds. He is a "mocking" bird. Sometimes he is called an imitator. He usually repeats a certain phrase of his song over and over again. And it is pleasant to hear, so pleasant that some people like to sit and listen to it for long periods of time.

There is a time when the mockingbird's sound changes however. It is when he becomes frightened or alarmed. When this happens, his sounds change to a very loud harsh noise.

The mockingbird is a very plain-looking bird. He is dull gray with white. He feeds on insects most of the time but likes fruit too. When the insects do not seem to be around, the mockingbird has his own way to find them. First he spreads his wings. Then he moves his long tail rapidly, all the time stirring up the air. With that, the insects suddenly come out of hiding and the mockingbird has all the food he wants.

The mockingbird is a good fighter. He protects his family well, keeping the enemies from near the nest.

You have someone who watches over you and protects you too. It is your family. God made mothers and fathers that way. They know what is good for you. They know what is bad too. The Bible says you should love your parents and obey them.

"Honor your father and your mother" (Exodus 20:12).

MOCKINGBIRD

Ostriches and Danger

The ostrich is the largest living bird. But it cannot fly the way other birds fly. It has long and thin legs, and they are very powerful, so it is a good runner. It can run up to forty miles an hour.

This bird is not a very colorful one, but it does have some very beautiful black feathers. Both its wings and tail are snowy white. The ostrich is best known for its long neck.

Not only is the ostrich large, but so are the ostrich eggs. They are six inches long and five inches wide. Do you know how big that is? Well, if you were to hold one of these eggs in both of your hands, you would not be able to cover it. It is much too big for that. One egg usually weighs about a pound and a half.

The ostrich is a very helpful bird. Because it has such a long neck, it can look around and see far into the distance. When it sees danger, it warns the other forest animals. When the ostrich is cornered, it can kick very hard and run very fast.

So this large bird not only spots dangers, but it can usually outrun many of its enemies too.

Do you remember the story of Jesus' birth? Herod wanted to have Jesus killed. But God, who can see everywhere, saw danger and warned Joseph to take the young child to another place.

God takes care of all His children. He loves them all; He loves you. Do you love Him?

"We ought . . . to show hospitality"
(III John 8).

OSTRICH

THICK-BILLED PARROT

Parrots and Sounds

What is the most popular of all birds? Do you know? It is the parrot. Many people like to have a parrot living in a cage in their homes. But most parrots are still found in the tropical countries.

There are many different kinds of parrots, about three hundred kinds. Some have feathers that are yellow and green. Others have red and blue feathers. There are even some parrots who are not colorful at all.

Parrots have large heads with small, bright eyes. They have hooked bills. Their wings are rounded and their neck is short. Parrots have short legs too. Two of the toes point forward and two point back.

When parrots are in their forest homes, they make loud screeching sounds. Some make sounds that are like a whistle; others have a high-pitched squeak.

Parrots like to eat seeds, buds, and other vegetable matter. They also like fruit and flowers. They use their feet to hold food. If the seed is too hard, they first crack it with their bills.

Parrots can copy the sounds of animals or people. They can make either laughing or crying sounds. But just because they can say a few words, and imitate the sounds, does not mean that they become people. They are still parrots.

Some people act and talk like Christians. But there is only one way that a person can become a child of God. That is by asking Jesus to take away sin. That is called being born again. Have you become God's child?

"You must be born again" (John 3:7).

Pelicans and Equipment

The pelican is a big, odd-looking bird. Many people think it is the biggest of all the flying birds. Some pelicans get to be more than seventy inches long. They can weigh up to twenty-five pounds.

Pelicans are strong fliers. Their legs are short and the feet are webbed. (That means there are no separate toes.) Their bills are different from any other bird. They are very long with hooks at the tips. On the bottom side of the bill there is a funny-looking pouch. It looks like a big, open pocket. The pelicans use this pouch as a net to scoop up fish and other food.

Pelicans live in warm, tropical climates. They always pick a place near rivers or lakes so they can find lots of fish. Pelicans can skim across the top of the water. When they spot fish, they swoop down under the water and attack their meal. Then with one quick gulp, they swallow the fish whole.

Yes, pelicans are good fishermen. Part of the reason is because God has given them such a good piece of equipment—the pouch. It works like a net in the water.

Not many fishermen use nets today. Most people use rods and reels. But in Jesus' time the men used nets. This was part of their equipment.

Jesus asks us to be fishermen too. He tells us that we should be fishers of men. And what is our equipment? It is the Bible—God's Word. And the Word of God is the best equipment we can have.

"The word of the Lord is right" (Psalm 33:4).

BROWN PELICAN

TRUMPETER

Trumpeters and a Trumpet Sound

Did you know there was a bird called the trumpeter? He isn't very big, but he has a long neck, a short curved bill, and legs that are rather long. The wings of the trumpeter are rounded, so some people think the trumpeter is humpback.

This bird has soft feathers. They are long and thick. He lives in the hot, humid weather. Trumpeters make their homes on the ground, and they often live together in big groups.

Trumpeters do not fly, at least not very often. The reason is that it is hard for them to do so. But they can run fast, even faster than a dog.

And what do they eat? Fruit and berries, mostly those from plants that are close to the ground. The trumpeter likes to take a bath in shallow water. After a bath, he lets the sun dry his feathers.

The trumpeter got his name because of the loud deep call that he makes. It almost sounds like a trumpet. This sound becomes even louder when the members threaten each other.

The Bible tells us about another trumpet sound. It will be heard when Jesus comes to take the Christians to heaven. Even those people who have died will hear the trumpet sound and they will come out of their graves. Then all the Christians from all over the world will be together with Jesus in heaven.

Oh, how wonderful.

"The trumpet will sound, the dead will be raised" (I Corinthians 15:52).

ROCK DOVE

Pigeons and Building

Did you know that there were about 255 different kinds of pigeons? They do not all look like that bird you see walking along the sidewalk of a busy street. Some are very brightly colored. Others are drab looking.

Pigeons sometimes perch in trees or, if they live in cities or towns, they are often seen making a nest on the edge of buildings.

Pigeons eat snails, worms, and caterpillars as well as seeds that are left on the ground.

When a pigeon drinks water, he does it very differently from other birds. Most birds drink and then lift their heads to let the water go down into the throat. But the pigeon simply sucks up the water.

Another way pigeons differ from many birds is that they do not make beautiful music. Pigeons only make a cooing sound.

The pigeon does not build a strong nest. He brings in twigs and roots that can be easily found around trees and buildings. So the nests are not always firm.

Jesus talked about two men who were building houses. One house was put on a good, strong foundation that was made of rock. Even when it rained and stormed, the building did not topple over.

Another man put up his building in the sand. As soon as it began to storm, the building rocked and swayed, and soon came tumbling down.

Jesus said that one man was wise and one was foolish. Do you know which one was wise?

*"**God's solid foundation stands firm**"* (II Timothy 2:19).

26

Robins and Knowing the Way

Almost everyone has seen a robin. This bird is almost as common as a sparrow in most parts of the country. Many people feel that when the first robin is seen, spring has arrived.

Robins are famous for the way they can pull worms out of the ground. No other bird can do it quite the way the robin does it. Their favorite food however, is not the worm. Robins are fruit and berry eaters. They also eat caterpillars, beetles, flies, snails, spiders, and wasps.

Robins, like most other birds, spend winter months in the south where it is warm. They start their trip back north as soon as the ice and snow begin to thaw. Sometimes another snowstorm hits while they are on their way. When this happens, the robins often return to the warmer climate for another short stay.

When these birds first leave their warm climate, and head for their northern homes, they start very slowly. Sometimes they only go about seventeen miles a day. Later, however, after they are used to traveling again, they will cover between one hundred and two hundred miles a day.

When they arrive, the mother bird builds the nest. She mixes mud with her beak and then shapes it with her bill and feet. She lines it with grass and roots.

ROBIN

When the weather begins to get cold again, the robins once again migrate. Isn't it wonderful that they know where to go to get back to their other homes?

The Bible tells us about a bird who left and came back too. It came from Noah's ark. Noah sent it out to see if the flood were over. The bird left and later came back to the ark without getting lost.

Birds were made by God and He gave them the ability to find their way as they do.

"God created . . . every winged bird"
(Genesis 1:21).

27

CANADA GOOSE

Waterfowl and Care

Waterfowl, like swans, geese, and ducks, can be found almost all over the world. The only place these birds do not like to live is where it is cold. They like to be where there is fresh water. They often look for places where there are lots of small lakes. They do this, because then they can go to the shoreline and find food.

When the weather begins to change, waterfowl leave the cooler area and search for a warmer place to live. Most of them are not very good at carrying things in their bills. So when they build their new nests, they look for materials that are nearby. That way it is easier to bring the twigs, leaves, and branches to the nest.

A mother bird never leaves her eggs uncovered. If she must leave the nest, she finds feathers and leaves and carefully covers the eggs. This is done for two reasons: first to keep them warm, and second to be sure no enemy spots them and tries to bring harm.

Most waterfowl do not have beautiful voices. Their sounds have been called grunts, hoots, honks, and coos. When a quack is heard, it almost always comes from the female bird.

Do you remember the story of Moses and his mother? Sure you do! Moses' mother did almost the same thing the waterfowl mother does. She hid her little baby by putting him in a basket. Then she put the basket in the water and had his sister watch him. This way she was sure he would live and be safe.

Jesus has promised to watch over us too. He said, "I will never leave you."

"I am watching over them" (Jeremiah 44:27).

Penguins and Walking

The penguin is known as a flightless bird. He has this name because he cannot fly. But he is a very good swimmer. He has strong muscles and a wide body. His so-called wings are flat. These are used as paddles when he is in the water.

Sometimes when the penguin is in the water he swims along gently. Other times he moves very, very quickly. Or he may dive under the water completely. He finds all of his food down in the water. He eats mostly fish.

Penguins live in the cool climate. Often hundreds of thousands of them can be seen living together.

Even though a penguin stands up straight like a person, he is a very clumsy bird. When he walks he wobbles around in a strange way. But God made the penguin to be what he is and to walk the way he walks.

And remember, God made you to be what you are; He made you to walk and run and to move around as you play. You see, God made everything and everybody. He made the little children with different colors of skin. He made their mothers and fathers too. These people may not look like you look. And you may not look like they look. But everything was made by our God.

God is so great. He made the penguin and He made people. But penguins cannot talk; they cannot pray to God. You can. So why not stop right now and tell God "thank you" for making you like you are. Tell Him that you love Him.

"God, you are very great" (Psalm 104:1).

ADELIE PENGUIN

Turkeys and Thanksgiving

What is your favorite special day? Is it Christmas? your birthday? or Thanksgiving? Many people think Thanksgiving is the most special day. They think about having a big meal, a meal that almost always includes a turkey.

A turkey is a big, powerful bird. He is bigger than a chicken. He has very strong legs. The turkey's head and neck are bare. He does not have feathers there.

Turkeys eat grain, seed, and berries. They eat insects too. Sometimes the male turkey likes to spread his tail into a beautiful fan shape. When he does this, he shows all the colors in it. A full grown male turkey is called a gobbler.

The turkey has many different sounds. These sounds are called clucks, yelps, gobbles, and gurgles. But one thing the turkey cannot do is sing.

The turkey has become a favorite and important food for Thanksgiving dinner. But even as important as the turkey is at Thanksgiving dinner, it is not the most important thing of the day. Thanksgiving is a time to remember all the good things God has given us. It is a time to say "thank you" for these things.

Some people never say thanks to God. They do not pray and they do not think about God. They make Thanksgiving day a time to invite company or go to someone's house. They think it is only a day to eat turkey.

There are many places in the Bible that tell us about thanksgiving. Some tell us to "sing" our thanks to God. And remember, singing is something the turkey cannot do. But you can.

"Sing to the Lord with thanksgiving" (Psalm 147:7).

WILD TURKEY

AMERICAN GOLDFINCH

Voices and God

Different birds have different sounds. Some of them are very musical. They sound like songs. Others are not musical at all. Their calls sound like noise.

Some birds have more than one kind of call. But all birds recognize the call of their own family. They know when there is danger. And they know when everything is all right.

Many bird lovers know different bird calls too. They have studied them and listened to them. When a bird begins to sing, these birdlovers can tell you which one it is. They can even imitate bird calls.

People have different sounds too. You can tell the difference between your mother's voice and your father's voice, can't you? One is low and one is high. If there are brothers and sisters in your family, you can tell which one is talking to you even without looking at them.

But you do not know the voices of every stranger, do you? Your mother and father do not know every person's voice either. But there is Someone who knows every voice in the whole world. It doesn't matter if it is the voice of a person, an animal, or a bird. He knows them all. Do you know who that is? Yes, it is God.

When you talk to God, (that is when you pray to Him) He knows your voice right away. He never gets you mixed up with any other boy or girl. He knows every voice in the whole, wide world. He knows when a little child in India, Africa, or America is talking to Him. Even if everyone all over the world talks at exactly the same time God hears and knows every voice. He is God and He knows everything. Have you talked to Him today?

"I lift up my voice to the Lord" (Psalm 142:1).

Sand Grouse and Water

The sand grouse is a bird that makes his home on the ground. He is about the size of a pigeon, but he has long, pointed, and very strong wings that help him in his long-distance flying.

The sand grouse likes to eat hard seeds. But he must also have lots of water. It is important for his diet. It softens the hard seed so he can digest it better.

Sometimes the sand grouse cannot find water nearby. When this happens, he goes farther and farther away to look for it. He has been known to travel fifty miles or more to find it. Then after he had drunk all the water he needed he had to travel the fifty miles back to his nest.

The baby sand grouse leaves his nest right after he is born. But since he is too young to travel very far for food and water, he needs help. His mother takes him out and shows him how to find food. His father goes after water and brings it back to him.

Water is very important for everyone. In the Bible we read about that strong man Samson. He needed water. He had fought hard and killed about one thousand enemies. After that hard job he was thirsty. But there was no water around. He prayed to God for water. He said, "You helped me to kill my enemies; now please don't let me die here of thirst."

God heard Samson's prayer and right there where he was standing, God made a well of water come up. Samson drank the water and his strength came back right away.

Everyone needs water in order to live. And Jesus says that everyone needs eternal water to live forever. Jesus is that water.

"Come all you who are thirsty" (Isaiah 55:1).

BLACK BELLIED SAND GROUSE

CEDAR WAXWING

Waxwings and Sharing

There is a very unusual bird called the waxwing. It has short legs, but its toes have long claws on them. Most waxwings have gray and tan feathers. But some are much more colorful. They have yellow and white wings. When they fly, even a red color shows up.

The waxwing likes to eat fruit and berries. When several waxwings sit together on a twig or branch where there are berries, they seem to play a sharing game. Whichever bird is nearest to the berries, takes a berry from the branch and passes it on to the next bird. Each bird down the line gives it to the next one until the tasty fruit has been shared by all of them. The waxwing is not selfish. He does not gulp down all the berries and leave the others to find their own food. He shares what he finds.

There is a beautiful story in the New Testament of the Bible that tells about a young boy who shared what he had. Do you know the story? It is sometimes called "the feeding of the five thousand."

Many people had come to listen to the teachings of Jesus. They had been there for a long time. By late afternoon they were hungry. Jesus knew this, so He told His disciples to give the people something to eat. The disciples found a little boy who had brought a lunch. The boy gave them his lunch and after Jesus blessed the food, it became enough to feed all those people.

Jesus cared about these people. He cares about you and me too. He cares about us much more than the waxwing cares for the other birds. Jesus cares because He loves us. He wants us to love too.

"Love comes from God" (I John 4:7).

WRYNECK

Wrynecks and Listening

The wryneck is almost like the woodpecker, except that he is only about six inches long. He makes his home in Europe and Asia while the weather is warm there. Then he migrates (travels) to India and Africa for the warmer weather.

This bird spends his time in the forest, usually on one of the upper branches of a tree. Just before he migrates to the warmer climate however, he can often be found down on one of the lower limbs of a bush or even on the ground.

The wryneck likes to eat insects, especially ants. Although his relative, the woodpecker, drills into a tree looking for food, the wryneck cannot do this. His bill is too weak to dig into the wood. Instead, he uses his long, sticky tongue to lick the insects from the bark of trees and branches.

For a nest, the wryneck usually looks for a ready-made hole in a tree. He does not gather leaves or twigs to cover this nest like other birds do. He uses it just as it is.

When the wryneck wants to protect his young, he makes a snake-like movement that frightens away the enemy.

And do you know why the wryneck was given such a strange name? Because he can twist his head around in all sorts of strange positions.

Sometimes when boys and girls are in church and Sunday school they twist and turn and move around just like a wryneck. Instead, they should listen to what the teacher or pastor is talking about. Yes, it is hard to sit quietly and listen, but we should learn to do so.

"Be still, and know that I am God" (Psalm 46:10).